What They Don't Teach You In Cosmetology School

The Uncensored Truth About What It Really Takes to Become an Expert Stylist, Make Great Money, and Control Your Own Future

Marquetta Breslin

RMNC Publishing

RMNC Publishing
10620 Southern Highlands Parkway Suite 110-18
Las Vegas, NV 89141

Printed in the United States of America

First published in 2019 by RMNC Publishing, a member of Breslin Products, LLC.

Book Layout © 2019 Capstone Design Group LLC

What They Don't Teach You In Cosmetology School / Marquetta Breslin – 1st Edition

ISBN 978-193502007-3

Contents

Dedicated to my customers, clients, and friends in the beauty industry

Why I Wrote This Book

No one goes into cosmetology school and says, "I can't wait to graduate and spend the rest of my life working far too hard for far too little." Yet, that's what happens to countless stylists and beauty professionals.

All over the country, beauty professionals struggle to make ends meet, struggle to fill their calendars with clients, and struggle to make a great living doing what they love. My intention for writing this book is to change that.

While cosmetology school is a great way to develop your skills for becoming a beauty professional, it does not give you the tools you need to thrive. Even worse, it trains you to think and act like every other stylist out there. It gives you "rules of the road" for the beauty industry that lead to a never-ending race to the bottom.

"Work hard, work your way up, stay humble, and pay your dues."

All of these ideas hold a kernel of truth. Unfortunately, if you follow the example you see put before you in cosmetology school about what it means to be a professional stylist, you will find yourself in a "work hard forever" rut that can easily turn the very thing you love doing most into a daily grind with no end in sight.

Remember this: there is a big difference between being a <u>great</u> stylist and a <u>successful</u> one.

The good news is that you can be great **and** successful. You can be what I call a **Million Dollar Stylist®**. That's what this book will help you do. What you will find in the following pages is a collection of real-world wisdom that you're not taught in cosmetology school.

This book is not about doing hair better. It's about completely transforming what it means to be a stylist. This is a transformation that's going to start in that valuable "real estate" located right between your ears. From there, it's going to spread into your physical reality.

As you read through this book, you might find things that surprise you or even make you angry. My suggestion is to take your time and go through it with an open mind. In fact, many of the ideas might run counter to what you've been told.

Consider this thought: look at the life of your "average" stylist. Why are so many talented people struggling? I'll tell you why. They're struggling because they were taught to believe things about what it means to make it in this industry that are simply not true.

Years ago, when I entered the beauty industry, I wish I were privy to the information I am sharing with you now. Cosmetology school taught me to do hair, not build a business. I suspect you've had the same experience. In this book I will teach you how to build a solid foundation for future success in the beauty industry. In fact, it's no accident that I limited the number of pages. I want you to finish this book in one sitting. That way you can take the information I am providing to you today and hit the ground running with it tomorrow.

Understand this:

You are here to make the world a more beautiful place. Here's my greatest hope for you—that you can share your gifts with the world and receive the abundance that comes from doing such valuable work.

We all have purpose and a reason for being. You're not reading this book by accident. You are meant to be right here, right now.

What you're about to read are 47 life lessons I wish someone would have shared with me when I first got started in the beauty industry. If I would have had a book like this years ago, it would have saved me so much time, money, and heartbreak.

My prayer is that these 47 lessons bless your life and your business. And never forget, even if you only take one or two ideas and make a change in your life, the time you've spent reading this book was worth it. Now let's get started!

The Journey Begins Now....

Remember this day. Write down the date somewhere so you will remember it because it's **this** day that's going to serve as a clear marker in your life and business. A year from now you're going to look back at **this** day and say, *"This is where it all changed for me...."*

Now make no mistake—the book you're holding in your hands isn't magic. It's not a silver bullet that's going to allow you to snap your fingers and have riches showered down upon you. That's not how success really works. It might look that way from the **outside** but when you're actually living it, it feels quite different.

While there's no genie that's going to pop up and make all your dreams come true, that doesn't mean what you're holding in your hands right now isn't powerful. It is. It's perhaps the most powerful tool currently available to stylists like you all over the world.

What you are holding in your hands is a roadmap. This is **not** a roadmap they give to you in cosmetology school. They teach you about hair. They don't teach you how to be successful. This roadmap will show you the way to a land very few stylists know exists. It's a land where even **fewer** stylists find themselves.

This land I'm talking about is what I call the world of the Million Dollar Stylist®.

Make no mistake, we Million Dollar Stylists® are not afraid of work. We believe that working hard and smart is the way to create success.

Your reality is formed by your thoughts, feelings, and beliefs about who you are and what you do.

But get this.... *like* attracts *like*. That means if you spend your days transmitting a signal that you hate what you're doing... that your clients drive you crazy... well, guess what you're going to get more of? You're going to get more annoyance, you're going to get more of the things you dislike, and crazy clients are going to come out of the woodwork!

This is how it works. I didn't make it up.

This is why so many stylists are working so hard without actually getting anywhere. You must continually focus on your thoughts, feelings, and beliefs about who you are, what you stand for, and what you believe.

This is the missing piece of the puzzle that 98% of stylists don't know.

Make no mistake. This is a **skill** that you will work on for the rest of your life.

Step 1 is to become aware of it. Just do that for the next seven days. Start **paying attention** to what you're thinking and feeling instead of getting 100% *caught up* in what you're thinking and feeling.

Be the observer. That alone will double or triple the amount of power you have in the world.

What Signals Are You Sending?

This is what you want to pay attention to. At first, you're probably not going to be good at this, but don't let that get you down. It's a skill, and skills take time to develop.

Imagine you wanted to drive yourself to the beach. You'd never just hop in your car without a map and start driving with your eyes closed. That would be crazy, right?

However, that's what stylists do all the time with their internal guidance system.

They're not even aware that they aren't paying attention to the "road." Becoming aware of your thoughts and feelings is the same as finally opening your eyes while you're driving down the road.

First, become aware of your feelings. Then you learn how to control them. When you are able to do that, you can shift your mindset to a more positive way of thinking instead of focusing on the negative.

Mind you, this doesn't happen instantly. That's not how it works. This isn't make believe. This is reality, so there's definitely a delay in the results.

That's why you turn this skill into a habit. When you develop the ability to consistently put out the signal of exactly what you want to attract, those things tend to show up!

2

Living Life by Design

Most stylists live their lives by **default**. They take what they get. They deal with it because they think it's the best they can do. This type of stylist doesn't like how things are going, but she keeps waking up every day anyway. It's slow, it's hard, and it's just not going to change at all.

This type of stylist is the one that tries to make ends meet by working all the time. She does it even though she's tired. She does it even though her feet hurt like crazy from standing so many hours. She does it even though she can't imagine this life being the rest of her life.

Yet, she still continues day after day. It's all the same. **"LIFE HAPPENS" to this stylist every single day**.

Then there's the Million Dollar Stylist®.

Million Dollar Stylists® **don't** live life by default. They live life **by their design**. That means they develop the skills to dream big, work smart, and live rich. This is quite a departure from average. Should you truly commit to walking this road, the people in your life are going to sit up and take notice.

"What is going on with you? You just seem... different," they'll say. If this starts to happen to you, don't worry! It's a big clue that you are moving in the right direction.

Our training in school was set up to make us feel terrible about feeling different. However, in real life, unless you are different and unless you are better, <u>you will be invisible</u>.

Therefore, you're going to make a very clear choice in your mind about which type of stylist you want to be. **Do you want to be one of "US?" Or, do you want to be one of "THEM?"**

I probably don't have to tell you that the future for the average stylist is <u>not</u> a bright one. It's full of an endless amount of low-level work. It's full of clients who will go somewhere else if your fees get too high. It's full of clients who just don't respect you and their behavior shows it.

The future for the Million Dollar Stylist® is totally different. If you commit to walking this road, you will enjoy a level of success that is simply amazing.

You will attract great clients who will pay your premium fees, and you will develop multiple streams of income so you won't even have to work with clients if you don't want to.

Like I've said, this is life by **design**. The hardest part, really, is just figuring out what type of life you want to live!

The first step is to simply make the decision that you're not going to settle for average. After all, is average what you really want?

3

You Get Paid for Solving Problems

Despite what you hear some people say, the beauty business is <u>not</u> about making money. I know that might strike you as something odd or even stupid to say but, really, it's the truth.

If money is the only reason you're playing this game of business, you're going to lose. In fact, you've already lost... unless you make a course correction... right NOW. Money isn't the goal here.

Money is the byproduct of the goal. Say that a few times so that you never forget it. This single shift in perception will make a big difference in your future.

So, if the point of business isn't money, what IS the point?

The point is to solve problems for people and make their lives better on many levels. If you do that, money tends to show up.

The first secret is to make sure you're focused on the right thing. You don't focus on money; you focus on real solutions for real people.

You can always tell when someone is just out for the money.

Something doesn't feel right when you deal with them. They can say all the right things and they can look a certain way, but you still notice there's something wrong.

That's because there IS something wrong!

Your gut knows it even if you can't figure out HOW you know it.

When someone's heart is in the right place, that comes through loud and clear too. It sends a clear message because the person you are talking to knows you actually have their best interests at heart.

That's what successful stylists do: we put the interests of our customers and clients before our own.

Trust me when I tell you that this path is the way to get everything you could ever want in life. You do it by making sure other people get what they want first.

Never forget that you get paid to solve problems.

4

Become a Servant

I guarantee this is not something you're going to read in a business book.

However, I feel strongly about this and I think, if you resonate with this idea, it can carry you a very long way, especially in today's world.

Most beauty professionals go into the world with the idea of trying to get what they want.

That's what we're taught to do, right? Go out there and make your dream a reality!

While there's nothing wrong with that, there is a slightly different (almost opposite) approach I think helps you play this game on a much bigger playing field. (Never forget it is a game. It makes it a whole lot more fun!)

Instead of asking yourself how to get what you want, start asking yourself how you can provide to **others** what *they* want.

From my perspective, this is the very foundation for your success as a stylist. It's about helping the people you work with to get what they want.

When you do that effectively, you can't help but to get what you want.

If you pursue what you want directly... if you pursue it first, you will leave a lot of money on the table.

Because people will know, and they'll realize you're just looking out for yourself.

Believe it or not, "looking out for yourself" is not the best way to get what you want.

Instead, here's a different habit to start and strengthen over time. You can do it each day.

Your daily thoughts need to be about how you can improve the lives of the people you help.

That's it. It's extremely simple. Ask how you can improve the lives of others, start looking for answers, and then take action on those answers.

Give up thinking about "ME, ME, ME," and start becoming a true servant of others.

5

This Little Light of Mine

There's ALWAYS going to be someone with more success, more possessions, a bigger house, more fans, more money, a shinier car, more shoes, and better nails. Always!

Therefore, to compare what you've got going on with anyone else will never be helpful.

You've got your unique path through life. Your experience will be unique.

When you spend a lot of time comparing yourself to others, your brain goes into story mode and makes up reasons why your life is or isn't the way it "should" be.

Not only is this a waste of your time, but it also takes your focus off the service you can provide to make the world a better place.

Comparing yourself to others is a dead end, but I want to talk about an even more damaging way to compare yourself to others.

This one doesn't get as much attention, but it can really mess with your head!

I'm going to talk about the comparisons you might make as YOUR life and success begin to take off while the other people around you just stay put.

Depending on how you were raised, this can make someone extremely uncomfortable.

You can't control what other people do. That's a fact. However, as you start growing, as you start improving, as you start walking on the road to success, people are going to notice.

Many times, those people are the ones who are closest to you.

They'll start noticing changes.... They'll start wondering why you're talking differently.... They'll start to feel a little bit uncomfortable with how you're acting.

At some point, they'll probably ask you this question: "What's going on with you?" This may make you feel uncomfortable. Here's why.

We were NOT trained to be OKAY with letting our light shine. We were trained to not want to make someone else feel "bad." First of all, that's not in our power to do. Second of all, that's crazy talk.

Listen up. I'm going to hit this one head on.

Choosing to shine your light of excellence as brightly as you can will never—can NEVER—diminish the light of someone else.

So please, choose to go out there and be the best that you can be. There are people in this world WAITING for you to show up for them.

If you are serious about this journey, people will wonder what's going on with you.

They'll wonder why you are changing. Just take a breath and keep going. Your life will be like a rose as it opens and blooms.

You should expect people to notice beauty like that.

6

How to Transform Your Life in 30 Days

Here is my challenge to you over the next 30 days.

Each morning when you wake up and each evening before you go to bed, breathe deeply for 10 minutes with your eyes closed. In your mind, I want you to start painting a picture of your life and business exactly as you want it.

At first, this might go very quickly. You might be done in two minutes but you're not done.... You're just getting started. Next, add more details. Make this movie of your "perfect" life as detailed as you possibly can.

Think about how things look, how you feel, how you act, how things smell—even what kind of weather is outside while everything is happening. No detail is too small. **In fact, it's the level of detail that really makes this work.**

This is the movie you are going to replay every morning and every evening before you go to bed.

That's really the most important part of all of this, but there's another step I want to mention as well. As you go through your day and things begin to happen, check in with what you are feeling and what you are thinking.

For example, let's say cash is tight and you were depending on that client to show up today. We've all been there.

How do you feel when that client *doesn't* show? How do you feel when that client calls ten minutes before her appointment and asks you to reschedule?

It doesn't feel good. An average stylist would take that feeling and just wallow in it for the rest of the day... or even the rest of the week.

She'd have no idea that her feeling was sending out a strong signal into the world to bring back MORE of that exact feeling.

The Million Dollar Stylist® doesn't behave like this. Sure, things happen that drive you crazy. But it's at that point where you get to make a choice.

You get to choose whether you take that thought or feeling and allow yourself to transmit it out into the world. Or... you get to choose to wipe it clean and re-center yourself on the feelings you have when you play your movie in your mind.

The real secret is to stop wanting and to start "behaving and feeling as if." That doesn't mean you start acting like a millionaire when you have $4.00 in the bank. It means that if you want to become a millionaire, you practice the habit of **feeling** like one now.

When you really start to become aware of what you're feeling and thinking and then look at what's going on in your life, you're going to be amazed at how this works.

If you really want to become a master of this, go to your favorite book store and find a copy of Maxwell Maltz's *Psycho-Cybernetics* book. It will take what I just told you to an entirely new level. Let me explain....

Maxwell Maltz was a plastic surgeon who started noticing a very bizarre trend in his work with clients. What he noticed was that even though his work made people look beautiful, after a short time his patients would resort back to the way they **used** to feel about themselves. In other words, all of his plastic surgery on the *outside* could never permanently change what the person was feeling and thinking on the inside.

That's when he started doing experiments. As a result, he created exercises just like the one I mentioned to you about the movie you play in your mind.

Dr. Maltz's creation is something that's been used by countless people to change their lives. Now the secret is in your hands. What will you do with it?

7

Step Up and Take Control

You're not going to change if you don't really want to change.

While most people think that changing habits is hard because change is hard, that's really not quite true.

The truth is that changing habits is hard because many people aren't honest with themselves about what they really want and don't want.

If you start trying to move toward a goal you really don't care about, you are not going to make it. That's just the 100% truth.

Lots of people say they want to be in shape, but they really don't want that. If they did, they'd actually do the things required to get there.

It's not right or wrong to want something. It's your life. You get to make these decisions for yourself.

However, if you want to set yourself up for success, then you owe it to yourself to be HONEST about what you really want and don't want.

You have to be honest with yourself and stop worrying about what others will think about your decisions. What others think about you is absolutely none of your business.

If you're used to living and working based on what you should do or what you think others think you should do, then figuring out what YOU actually want to do might be a challenge!

Sometimes there's so much mental chatter going on in your head that it can take a while before it starts to calm down. Most of us were trained to live for other people. We were trained to live for their approval, for their validation, and for their acceptance of what we do.

This is a hard road, and it can make it a real challenge to figure out what you actually want, yet that's where we have to get to.

Get clear on what you really want. Take your time. This isn't a race. It's your life! You owe it to yourself to do it right.

Once you start to get clear on what it is you want, or even get a glimpse of that, then you can start to make decisions that make sense for you. Otherwise, you're just flying through life and business without being able to truly see.

Is there something in your life right now that you actually want to change?

Is there one thing you can think of that you are going to get rid of?

Or is there something that you'd like to add that is actually important to you?

8

Moving out of the Victimhood Zip Code

This lesson is not for the average stylist. The average stylist is happy to be the victim in his or her life.

Why does victimhood pay off? It's because they can give themselves a way to take the responsibility for their situation off themselves and put it on someone else.

"They did this to me! If it weren't for them, I'd be more successful."

"If only this would stop happening, then I'd have a chance to get somewhere."

Do these comments sound familiar? Do you know what all these statements have in common? These are excuses that people use to keep from doing the one thing that scares almost everyone to death.

What is that thing?

TAKING RESPONSIBILITY FOR EVERYTHING IN THEIR LIVES.

Fear shows up for you as the perfect teacher you need, in the perfect way, at the perfect time. It changes shape, size, color... everything... based on what you need.

Let's say you always have people around you who complain that you aren't doing enough for them. Maybe some of them embarrass you or talk to other people about how you "let them down."

Most people would put on the victim hat in that situation and start fighting back.

Million Dollar Stylists® would do something very, very different.

Million Dollar Stylists® would understand that these folks are the people for whom you should be giving thanks because they are serving the role of messenger to bring you the lessons you need to grow.

If you don't get the lessons, they keep showing up.

Look at all the annoying situations in your life and business—where the same stuff just keeps happening again and again—and ask yourself a simple question:

What Is the Lesson I'm Supposed to Learn?

When you start asking insightful questions like this one, then you will go places because over time you're going to start figuring out what these lessons are for you. Then you're going to work on them and learn them and master them.

When they are resolved, they will stop coming.

Then what's going to happen?

Life will give you more lessons but only because you're ready for them. *That's why we're here*—to become the best versions of ourselves that we can possibly be. Most importantly, don't worry that you're never "done" learning.

Finishing isn't the point. Getting better is the point.

9

Own It

I'll be the first to admit that this is probably the hardest step of all; however, it's the most important one.

Because most of us were trained to consistently wish we were somehow different than we actually are.

It's like a disease that adds absolutely no value to our lives.

I wish I were richer.... I wish I were thinner.... I wish I were more successful.... I wish I had the life [insert someone's name] has.... I wish I had more time.... I wish I had a better job.... I wish I had a better business.... I wish I were more [insert whatever you want] ....

This is a crazy thing to do to yourself. Yet, we all do it.

Going through life like this is a great way to be miserable.

And it's definitely ONE habit you might consider putting on your list for a serious transformation.

Read that again. This mental chatter is nothing more than a **habit**.

But it's a big one because most of us have practiced this more than every other habit we have combined!

So, what do we do with it?

How do we move beyond this "nothing will ever be good enough, right enough, perfect enough" disease that infects everyone's mind?

Here's how—if you want to end one habit, you must replace it with a better habit. Instead of allowing that mental chatter to flow uninterrupted in your mind, you take control of it.

The next time it starts to take over and tell you why your life will be better when..., just say **STOP**.

And then say, "I am so grateful for everything in my life right now. I am grateful for now, grateful for things just as they are **now**."

This doesn't mean you're not growing. It doesn't mean you don't have goals. It doesn't mean that your future isn't going to be on a totally different level than your present situation.

What it does mean is that you are thankful for the process of growth you're experiencing **now**.

If you actually want to be happy while you're growing and getting better, then this is the habit you want to install—the habit of constant gratitude.

You be must thankful for the life God has given you. Start now.

I can't stress enough how important this decision is to your life and overall well-being.

This is the one habit that will really make all of the difference in the quality of your journey.

It's probably not surprising that not too many people master this one.

That's how you can have millionaires and other extremely "successful" people still be totally miserable.

It's because they thought things would be different once they "made it."

However, that's just a lie they tell themselves. If you can't be happy now, you're never going to be happy.

Being happy is a decision. It's a habit too.

Let me share a story with you, my story about choosing to be happy. Years ago, when Ricky and I were still Active Duty Air Force, we received orders to get stationed in Charleston, SC. At first, we were excited. We couldn't wait to get there and start our new lives.

Once we arrived and got settled in, I realized how much I *didn't* like Charleston, SC. In fact, I didn't like it at all. When people asked if I liked it there, I'd say, "I'm ready to move back to Virginia. I'd drop everything right now and move if given the opportunity."

In fact, it took me a few years to really settle into the Charleston way of living. Once I did, I made a mental decision to love it—not just like it but LOVE it! I realized at that moment that you have to decide to be happy and constantly work at it. However, it's a habit that you must develop.

It's a habit of thinking and being and trusting God.

10

Invisible Programs That Rule Your World

Let's take a little trip back in time to a point in your life where someone was clearly not pleased with you—maybe it's a client who didn't like what you did to her hair, maybe it's a teacher from school.

I'll quickly share a situation that happened to me years ago. I received a referral from a regular client, which is, of course, always appreciated. This referral was for a full head of extensions, and I felt pretty good about it.

The prospective client—we'll call her Jane—came in excited. Jane took a seat and began to explain to me her concerns about her hair. It was paper thin and I knew going in it would be a challenge, but I was very confident that I had a solution to suit her needs.

As with any style, I let her know the pros and cons, AND I also explained to her my money-back guarantee. She was still excited and wanted to move forward, but she couldn't afford to move forward right then so she paid little by little until she had paid in full.

Once she paid in full, I scheduled her appointment and it was on. She showed up for the appointment, and I did her entire head of extensions. It took about four hours for the entire process.

When I spun her chair around to look in the mirror, she burst into tears of joy! She couldn't believe it was her. She hugged me, looked in the mirror, hugged me again, and then went right back to the mirror. She was so excited!

I received a text a few days later saying how much she loved her hair. I was so happy for her! Then, the next day, I received a text from Jane that shocked me. Her text said she hated her hair and so did everyone else around her. She said she felt ugly and wanted it out. I looked at the calendar, and it was the last day of her promised money-back guarantee.

What did I do? I scheduled an appointment to take out her extensions. I've got to admit that when she arrived, the space between us felt "weird." Nonetheless, I fulfilled my three-day-money-back guarantee, removed her hair, and gave back every penny. It was an icky feeling.

Now it's your turn.

Go back to that negative situation in your past and RE-LIVE it in slow motion. However, instead of putting yourself back in your body, just watch as you and the other person re-live the scene.

At some point, you're likely to recall some of the negative feelings you've experienced. In fact, you probably won't have too much trouble bringing that fear right back into your gut. It's a terrible feeling, I know. I've experienced it many times.

The reason I'm asking you to go back and pull up this feeling is because I actually want you to feel it again. Now that time has passed from the original event, you can use this experience to take a major step forward.

OKAY, so you've got this weird feeling in your gut.... Now what? Just sit there with it. Don't try to get rid of it. Don't try to do anything. Just sit there and feel it.

Understand this principle: fear is the enemy... period.

When undesirable feelings arise, the mind tends to kick in and create a story around that negative energy that we think means something.

For instance, let's say you've finished your client's hair and she starts to cry... except she's not crying tears of joy. She doesn't like her hair, and now she thinks she looks awful.

Then she turns to you and tells you this is the worst experience she's ever had and she's never coming back. Nobody likes stuff like this to happen, BUT this is the reality: sometimes people won't like what you do. Sometimes people just won't like you, period.

When you feel this fear... the fear of rejection... or the fear of being made fun of... or the fear of knowing someone doesn't like you... you have a choice.

You can either do what most people do, or you can learn to approach this like a real Million Dollar Stylist®.

Most people, when faced with fear, trigger one of their automatic and invisible programs they've been running their entire lives.

When I say "program," I mean something similar to the thing that is used in a computer. Programs are instructions that tell a computer what to do. Think of your brain as a computer. We have programs, too, except we're running our programs most of the time without even being aware that they are there.

The average person, when faced with fear, is going to run one of these programs. They will react, and that reaction will be automatic.

It looks something like this....

> » Some people's programmed response is to start apologizing.

> » Others get defensive and start arguing why the other person is wrong.

> » Some will just break down and start blabbing on and on about what a hard day it's been and how difficult life is.

We all have these programs, even Million Dollar Stylists®. The question is... do you want to continue to allow them to run your life?

If not, you must start changing them. However, before you can do that, you must start noticing them.

One way to do that is to stop reacting to things so quickly. When something happens, take a breath and check in. Ask yourself, "What is the best thing to do for the good of everyone?"

Remember that doing the "best thing for everyone" includes you too!

Keep in mind that no one is going to remind you how powerful you are. You have to remind yourself. One of the powers you have is to control which programs you will allow to remain in your mind and which ones you will throw in the trash.

If it's not serving you or helping you serve others, get rid of it!

The Other Golden Rule

Do you know the difference between bragging and exuding confidence? To brag is to raise up yourself to put others down. Confidence is raising yourself up so that you can raise up someone else too.

We can't give to others what we don't have for ourselves. That's why paying attention to caring for yourself is so important. You want to "fill yourself up" so that you can allow all that goodness to flow into the world and affect other people.

For many people, this is the exact opposite of what you were taught. And frankly, depending on how deep your habits are ingrained, this may take a bit of work to change.

We've all heard of the Golden Rule. "Do unto others as you would have them do unto you." That's a powerful rule to live by. However, there's another rule that's equally as powerful. You could think of it as the "other" Golden Rule.

This one is a little bit different. It says, "Do unto yourself as you would do unto others."

Read that again carefully, and give some thought to what that actually means and whether or not you've been living it.

The fact is, most people treat themselves far worse than they would ever dare treat another person. When you start treating yourself with more care and love, you can't help but do the same for others. Everyone wins in a situation like that.

12

When You Chase Clients, They Will Run Away!

Wouldn't you run away if someone were chasing you? Of course, you would! I would too.

However, this is exactly what most stylists do. They might not think they are chasing clients, but they are.

After all, how do you get clients if you don't TRY to get clients?

You attract them.

You don't go to them. They come to you! You'll never hear this approach talked about in cosmetology school. They can't teach it because they don't even know it exists! And they certainly don't know how to do it. If you've ever heard that you should "start at the bottom and work your way up," that's a clue you're talking to someone who has no idea there's a much better, more fun, and more profitable way to go about creating success as a stylist.

Think about the things that stylists do to get clients. They discount their services. They never stop talking about "what they can do" for their clients.

While those stylists might think they are actually contributing to their future success, I look at that and know they are doing the exact opposite. If you want clients who treat you like garbage and haggle over what you charge, what I just mentioned is exactly how you get them.

That's not the type of client I'm looking for. I want the client who chooses me over and above all their other choices.

I want the client who has the resources to invest in getting the best I have to offer. I want the client who treats me like the expert. I want the client who trusts my advice and the vision I have for her hair.

If that's the type of client you want, then you're in the right place. However, understand this: that client doesn't just show up by chance.

You have to make it happen. You have to engineer what you do and how you do it so it can happen over and over again.

At this point in your journey you might not think this is possible, but it is. I know. I've lived it, and I help beauty professionals all over the world live it too.

Your first question might be **how** to do that. However, that's the wrong place to start. The journey begins with a total transformation inside of you.

Stop asking, "How do I get clients?" Instead, ask this powerful, life-changing question: "How can I serve people today to add value to their lives?"

13

Be a Leader TODAY

In cosmetology school we're taught to "put in your time" and to "work your way up."

The problem with this thinking is that it trains you to wait for someone else to tell you that you've made it.

This is backwards. Stop waiting. Choose yourself.

The truth is, you can be a leader **TODAY**. You can be someone your clients respect **TODAY**. You can be a trusted advisor **TODAY**.

Now, this is my approach. Surely, you'll find plenty of business advice telling you it's all about the money but let's get real. When we come to the end of our journey in this life, money is going to be way down on the list of things that are important. If you see how obvious it will be then, why not use that knowledge to your advantage now?

What you're really doing when you're leading is this: you're sending a promise into the world. That's why people get inspired and empowered by leaders. Their actions communicate it, whether or not they say it out loud.

What's my promise for Million Dollar Stylist®? It's that every single interaction with me is going to leave you better than before.

I guarantee that if you make that same promise to your clients, your world is going to transform. The best part is that you don't need anyone's permission to do this.

You just start.

14

It's Not About YOU.... It's Never About YOU

Humans are pretty self-centered little creatures. I'm not saying that's bad. I'm just saying that's how we're wired. Everyone is pretty much thinking about themselves most of the time.

That's why, if you can develop the habit to place your focus on others, you'll stick out like a sore thumb... in a good way! Who doesn't love being the focus of another person? I haven't met anyone yet.

The story you are going to tell must be focused on the people you are trying to attract.

The more you understand these people (their thoughts, their feelings, their fears, their hopes, their dreams), the better your story will be.

Once you get clear that this story is not about you, then you can start to piece it together.

The beginning of the story is about where your prospective clients and customers are right now. The second part of the story is about where they'd like to be.

You become the vehicle your people take to get where they're trying to go. This is the moral of the story!

15

Customer Lifetime Value Formula

This is really what separates the amateurs from the pros. The pros realize that nothing is free, so they don't spend a lot of time trying to get things for free. It's simply not worth it.

Usually "free" things do require payment. They just require payment in things other than money. Often times, the payment is in the form of time.

As a Million Dollar Stylist®, time is the most precious thing you have. As you go on this journey, the value of your time is going to go up. You must start treating it as the valuable treasure it is!

When I talk about paying for a client, I mean payment in the form of the marketing materials and systems you create.

The stylist who understands the lifetime value of a client is not afraid to invest some of that money UPFRONT to win that client.

That is the game right there. To win that game you need systems, and you need to pay attention. You don't want to just wing it like most stylists do.

Now, don't get overwhelmed by the details. Just because I'm teaching them doesn't mean you have to do them all at once.

This is a journey. That means it takes time. That means you're going to make mistakes. And that means you are going to pick yourself up over and over again and keep going.

That's not a problem. That's the point. Don't get discouraged.

Here's the main point I'm trying to etch into your mind. I'll ask it in the form of a question:

If you knew that a client was worth $3,000.00 to you over their lifetime and you could "buy" that client for $400.00 through your marketing materials, how many clients would you buy? The answer is that the smart stylist would buy as many as she could afford.

These are the numbers you're going to start discovering in your own business. The first one you can start with is Customer Lifetime Value.

Pick a repeat client. Go back and look at all of the work you've done for that client. Add it up and look at that amount.

Now do that for a few more clients. You're trying to end up with an average number you can keep in your head as you're building your marketing systems.

That's the number you'll keep in mind when new clients walk through the door.

16

How to Do Less and Accomplish More

Vilfredo Pareto was an Italian engineer who lived in the 1800s. How could this guy possibly make your life and business better today? It's because he discovered something interesting. You might even call it a universal law because the same law seems to repeat itself over and over again in just about every part of life and business. You'll want to live by his findings.

His discovery is referred to as The Pareto Principle. According to Wikipedia, here's what it is: "The Pareto principle (also known as the 80-20 rule, the law of the vital few) states that, for many events, roughly 80% of the effects come from 20% of the causes." You may be wondering, "What exactly does that mean?"

It means that 80% of the income is made by 20% of the people. It means that 20% of the people own 80% of the land.

Now, let's bring this principle into the world of the stylist.

It means 80% of your income generally comes from 20% of your clients.

It also means that just 20% of the effort you are investing to build your business is responsible for 80% of the results. And the flipside is also true: that 80% of your effort is creating a mere 20% of your results.

Read that last sentence again. It means that 80% of your effort is only generating 20% of your results.

So, if you get rid of that 80% of effort, you lose 20% of your results... but you free up 80% of your time!

80% of the inputs connect to 20% of the outputs.

This same phenomenon happens all over the place. If you start to pay attention to things and even measure them, you will notice this happening all around you.

Now the important thing to remember is the main point behind this principle. The main point is that a small number of inputs create the majority of the outputs. Maybe it's an 80% to 20% relationship, but it could be 90% to 10% just as well. The exact numbers don't matter. It's the point that matters.

How do you use this? You use this in your life and business to consistently improve the results you are getting while decreasing the effort you are investing to get those results.

This is a process that never ends. The result? Over time, you get increasingly more effective.

What happens if you get rid of the clients who are taking up 80% of your time but only paying you 20% of your money?

What happens if, now that you've freed up 80% of your time, you go out and find more of the "20% percent clients" who pay you really well?

I'll tell you what happens. You make more money with less effort. You have a better day. You don't get so run down. You feel like you are actually making progress in your business.

You feel this way because that's exactly what is happening!

No one in cosmetology school is going to tell you that firing clients is a good thing but I will! Not everyone is a good fit for you. If you spend time with the wrong people, you're never going to get where you want to go.

I still remember the first time I came across this principle. Now, I'm an organized person by nature, but when I started applying the 80/20 Principle to my life and work, the results were off the charts.

Living the Million Dollar Stylist® journey is about smart work, not hard work.

The 80/20 Principle is one of the most powerful things you can put in your toolkit to make sure you're always on the road to working smart.

17

Silence Is Power

Have you ever been caught in one of those extremely uncomfortable conversations that is so awkward it just makes you cringe? Maybe the other person has no social skills, or maybe there's just a weird vibe. Either way, the conversation is full of awkward pauses, and it just never goes anywhere.

Make no mistake—silence makes people uncomfortable... really uncomfortable. In fact, what usually happens in a conversation where the silence gets a little too long is that the person who can stand it least will jump in to say something. They'll do it just to break the silence!

My recommendation to you is to get used to that feeling. Just be OKAY with it. No one is going to die, even though it might feel like that the longer the silence goes on.

When you are the one who is asking questions, be OKAY with the person not responding right away. Just ask your question, and then close your mouth and wait.

This is an excellent tip if you ever find yourself in a negotiation. Imagine you're buying a car. You walk on the lot, and the salesperson runs over to you. All you say is something like, "I want that car, and I'm prepared to pay $X for it...." And then you just close your mouth and wait.

The first person to speak next loses. Really! This is how it works. The person who can't stand the silence will generally jump in and say something stupid, only because they are so uncomfortable.

Be prepared for that response so you don't get surprised. Silence is OKAY. In fact, many times, silence is power.

18

Ignore Your Weaknesses

The way we're brought up has this odd focus on trying to make you better at the things that don't come easily for you.

That's what you work on in school. That's what we're all trained to think about.

I'd be better if only I could "[INSERT WHATEVER IT IS THAT YOU AREN'T GOOD AT]."

When this is what you focus on, you miss seeing and developing the gifts you've been given to share.

Can you imagine asking an elephant to climb a tree? What if that elephant spent all of its energy trying to become a good tree climber?

What if it invested hours and hours working on its "weaknesses" so that it could compete with the monkeys?

What if the elephant's parents got called in to speak with the climbing instructor to talk about getting it some extra help with climbing?

Doesn't this sound nuts? It is. And this is the exact same thing human beings do.

It would be a little bit like walking over a huge pile of pennies and focusing ONLY on those without mentioning the big gold bars that were scattered throughout the pile.

Again, crazy!

Take a look at the gifts and talents you have. Pick one or several to develop. Then go to work!

That's your head start. What comes easily to you and what you're good at are clues that these are the things you might want to spend your time doing.

Don't do the things you're not good at. Don't do the things you don't enjoy.

Get creative and figure out a way to get those things out of your experience. Get someone else to do them, or figure out a way to make them unnecessary.

The most important point is this one:

Forget about your so-called weaknesses. Those don't matter. I wish I could stress to you how little they matter.

It's hard to believe, though, because of the depth of the training we've received that we should only focus on these things we aren't so good at.

You are here to be great. You are here to be powerful. You are here to add value to people's lives all over the world.

Focus on the tools you've been given to do that in its fullest form to be great and powerful. Nothing else matters.

19

You Will Be an Easy Target

As Million Dollar Stylists®, we are going places.

We have a destination on which we are focused.

We are walking our way to the land of the Million Dollar Stylist® where we get to enjoy certain life and business benefits that are not available to your average stylist.

This simple fact puts you in an elite group of people.

Most people have no goals, no plan, and no strategy for much of anything except getting to the couch by the time the sun goes down.

If you're actually going somewhere... if you're actually on a mission to achieve something important... you're going to be an easy target for people.

They're going to see you doing your thing, and there's a good chance it's going to rub some of them the wrong way.

There could be a lot of reasons for this, but one of the most common is that you're going to provide a mirror for them.

And it's a mirror that's going to show them what they *could* have and who they *could* be.

Just imagine if you spent the last five years eating nothing but cake while sitting on the couch 24 hours a day, seven days a week—nothing but cake!

That's going to lead to a certain state of things, physically speaking, and it most likely won't be pretty.

Your body will not be in an optimal state.

Imagine a group of people show up to your house. These people are BEAUTIFUL.

They have beautiful bodies. They've obviously been working hard, eating right, and reaping the benefits of those choices.

Unless you are very secure in your choice to be cake crazy, these folks will remind you of everything you COULD HAVE BEEN but chose not to be.

Now this example is pretty silly, but the point is the same.

As a Million Dollar Stylist®, you've made a commitment to do the work required to live and work on a level that others COULD be at but won't be at.

Most people don't want to become a Million Dollar Stylist. They only want to already be one.

We all know that's not how this works. It doesn't work unless you do.

Part of the price you pay on this journey is that you're going to run into people who want what you have but aren't willing to work hard enough to get it.

They aren't willing to focus. They aren't willing to fail. They aren't willing to endure the criticism of others.

They aren't willing to wade across the deep waters to the promise land.

As silly as it sounds, when they see you doing all of these things and more, it can really frustrate them.

What do you do about it? Just be aware of it. Every time something like this happens, know it's only because you're making **real** progress on your journey.

20

Thou Shalt "Show" Not Tell

You want to learn the greatest undisclosed business building tactic I've ever seen?

It's simple: evidence of real results that you've helped your clients and customers create sells better than everything else combined!

You know those infomercials that play on TV where the guy gets out a permanent marker from a rug by spraying it with some type of goop?

He doesn't just sit on a chair and talk about how great the goop is. Instead, he **shows** you.

Say this a few times and really internalize it: the point is to SHOW not just TELL.

It's a simple, clear, and powerful route to success. It also separates the amateurs from the pros.

Why? It's because if you're going to leverage the power of SHOWING, that means you have to actually have something that works.

Do you? The answer is either a yes or a no. Don't freak out if you can't answer yes right now.

The answer you give right now doesn't control the rest of your life. It is simply a snapshot as things are right now.

You are either offering something to the marketplace that works or something that does not work.

The answer right now doesn't matter as much as what your answer is going to be in the near future.

In other words, are you doing the work required to get something that works, or are you just trying to figure out how to sell what you have? Now, all of us have to start somewhere. When I started, I had no results. I had just started. I had no results to show... yet. You do what you have to do.

In that case, you start with a pure heart, a clear mind, and a real desire to help people. Those are pretty valuable assets if you use them correctly.

If you're just starting out and you don't have proof that what you offer creates real results, that's fine.

Here's the good news. You've just finished your to-do list without even trying, and the only thing on that list is your new #1 priority:

Your number one priority is to get results for your clients, and then tell the world about those results!

The real goal is **<u>proof</u>** that you help your customers and clients create real results.

Once you are able to create that proof, then you build the machine that collects and distributes the proof to the rest of the world.

21

The Problem With ONE

Dan Kennedy, a businessman and marketer from whom I've learned a lot, has a simple saying. It goes something like this: "One is the worst number."

Kennedy has been in business for a long time. He's witnessed a lot of ups and downs.

This saying of his isn't talking about BEING #1 or anything like that.

What he means when he refers to "one" is that there's a serious problem with having ONE of anything: one idea, one plan, one business, one source of income, one source of new leads, one source of clients, one product, one service. It's a risky position to have only ONE. Get it?

If you have only ONE of anything, you're only one small disaster away from having nothing.

Most people would rather not think about things like this. The problem with this "non-thinking" is that these people eventually find themselves totally unprepared when challenges inevitably show up.

My goal for you is to never be in that position.

This "one of anything is a bad thing" rule is so important for Dan that, often, his first question in response to hearing someone's idea for a product/service/business is to ask, "What's your Plan B when that doesn't work out? What's Plan C when Plan B doesn't work?"

Are you beginning to see a pattern here?

Inexperienced business people go into business hoping that things are going to work out perfectly. Then, when things don't go according to plan, their hopes get crushed and they quit.

This happens thousands and thousands of times every week to businesses of all shapes and sizes. This is why so many businesses fail. It's because they weren't built to succeed!

If you're going to be a Million Dollar Stylist®, understand that you're going to run into challenges.

You're going to try things that don't work; you're going to have clients that drive you crazy; and you're going to make products no one wants.

The goal isn't to avoid these things because that's pretty much impossible.

The goal is to prepare for these things so you are ready for anything.

22

You'll Never Get There

This is going to sound crazy, but it's also really going to make you think. It's something that can help you break through to a whole new level of success.

For all we talk about getting to the beautiful land of the Million Dollar Stylist®, I have some news for you. At first, it's going to sound like bad news, and then I'm going to show you why it's good news.

The news is that you're never going to reach the land of the Million Dollar Stylist®. It's just never going to happen. Sorry.

It's not because you're not smart or talented or deserving of success, though. It's not going to happen for you because it's not supposed to happen for you. It's not going to happen for me, either. The fact is, there is no ultimate **DESTINATION** on this road.

The land of the Million Dollar Stylist® is a destination that is always just out of your reach, no matter how successful you become. That's the point. That's why it works. Because it provides for you the vision and the energy to become better tomorrow than you are today. When you do that enough days in a row, you will be amazed at the success you achieve.

This is a journey that never ends. That's not a bad thing! That's why, in the months and years to follow, you will be able to look back on your steps and be completely wowed by the progress you've made. Instead of hitching your wagon to the idea that you are someday going to "get there," start getting in the habit of committing to the way a Million Dollar Stylist® thinks, speaks, and acts **TODAY**. Embody that ideal and get to work.

The fact is, you can be a Million Dollar Stylist® NOW. You can do it today. Then you can do it again tomorrow and the day after that. That's the commitment you make... to do it TODAY. When you give up on the idea of ever getting anywhere, you are free.

You are free to focus your time and effort on the only thing we truly have: THE MOMENT YOU ARE LIVING RIGHT NOW.

The journey of the Million Dollar Stylist® is about breaking through just about every single limit you thought you had for your life and business. You don't do this all at once. You do it in small steps, repeated on a consistent basis. The secret is to be found in the habits you develop. First you must become aware of the habits you currently have. Then you must begin to change them and replace the habits that keep you from success with the ones that lead you closer to it.

Most people develop habits that keep them stuck. They do this because that is what they see others around them doing too. They develop habits that keep them feeling comfortable and safe. Unfortunately, those same habits also ensure they will never truly become the best version of themselves.

You are not here to be like those people. You are here for something better. You are here to be better. Everything you've ever wanted is out there waiting for you to bring it closer to you. Your habits will determine whether you get all those things or not.

23

Do You Want to Pay the Price?

There's one thing probably just about every stylist can agree on. Life is better when you have a steady stream of high quality clients coming through your door. Unfortunately, we learn absolutely nothing about how to do this in cosmetology school. In fact, what we are taught there actually works against us ever figuring out this piece of the success puzzle.

Cosmetology school teaches you to think, speak, and act just like every other average stylist out there. Now, there's nothing inherently wrong with this. You can still help people. However, being an average stylist means you are choosing to pay the price required to play that game.

The price I'm talking about is paid in the form of low fees, a lack of respect from clients, a feeling you always have to work hard to make ends meet, and more. To be blunt, it's not a fun way to go through life—not when you can hop on the Million Dollar Stylist® road and take that journey. That's a journey that brings you to an entirely new level of result.

Here's the bad news, if you can call it that. The Million Dollar Stylist® journey has a price too. We all have to pay that price. The price isn't paid in low fees or annoying clients, though. It's paid in time to learn and master your craft, energy to focus on improving yourself, and the dedication to build a system that powers your journey. Don't let anyone tell you otherwise. Nothing in life is free. You always pay for it somewhere.

The real secret is to figure out what you want from life and then make the decision about whether or not you are willing to pay the price for that.

24

Giving Up the "Need" for Clients

This is important, so please take your time as you read through this part. The goal of life isn't to rush through it to the end. The goal is to get as much as you can from every step of your journey.

If you want to get on the road to becoming a Million Dollar Stylist®, then you have to understand there is a fundamental difference between how you will go about getting clients and how an average stylist will go about getting clients. This is one of those mind shifts where just a single moment of "getting it" could transform your future in major ways.

The average stylist **needs** clients. Now technically, we all need clients, but the average stylist REALLY needs them. By that, I mean that she is filled with the feeling of need. This is a feeling that she broadcasts into the world to almost everyone she meets. It's especially strong when she feels like she is talking to someone who could be her client.

I imagine it's not too difficult to think of someone in your life who always needs something from you. Every time you see them, they ask you to do something for them. These people are not fun to be around. This is the kind of need I'm talking about that the average stylist embodies when it comes to getting clients. They need them.

The feeling of need is so great that they are willing to work for peanuts, they are willing to be treated like dirt, and they are even willing to completely inconvenience everyone around them to accommodate the client who can never show up on time. Remember, the average stylist needs clients. In response to that need, the average stylist will go out and chase those clients until she catches one.

The Million Dollar Stylist® doesn't do any of this. In fact, the Million Dollar Stylist® doesn't even view clients as something to get. Clients are people you attract not chase. Clients are not people who you hunt down. Clients are people who are hunting **YOU**. You may or may not believe that this is possible, but I'm here today to tell you that it is possible. I know.

25

Systems Riches for Stylists

Most stylists spend a lot of time and energy trying to get clients. While they think this is the route to success, the journey is rarely what they think it's going to be. The main reason for this is because spending time getting clients is going to trap you into doing some pretty hard work for the rest of your life. Here's why.

You'll always be looking for the next client. You'll always be wondering what you should do next to get that next person into your chair. So, what does a Million Dollar Stylist® do that's different? The short answer is that we have a completely different goal when it comes to client attraction.

Instead of going out there and getting the next client, we focus our time, energy, and effort on building a **SYSTEM** that attracts the client. Robert Kiyosaki (of *Rich Dad, Poor Dad* fame) tells a story that illustrates this point clearly:

Imagine a man who opens a business carrying water from the stream to the village. Each day, he wakes up and picks up his bucket. He walks to the stream, fills his bucket, and returns to the village to sell his water. Each day, this is the process he repeats. He is paid well for this service. Obviously, he is only paid upon delivery of his water. Without his bucket and effort, he generates zero income. This man is like the average stylist trying to get clients.

Kiyosaki then goes on to tell the story of another water worker—one that does his job in a completely different way. The funny thing about this water worker is that he never picked up a bucket... not even once. Instead, when he decided to add value to the community by delivering water, he went to work building a PIPELINE. The first day he put down a single pipe. The next day he put down another pipe. It took him months to build the pipeline. During that time, he didn't deliver one drop of water to the community.

He could have carried buckets at least half the day but he chose not to. Instead, he focused all of his energy on the pipeline. Finally, after many hours invested in the pipeline, it was ready to go. He flipped the switch and water began to flow. From that day forward, the community was happy to receive a constant flow of water for which they paid the man. Instead of spending his time delivering water, he spent his time building a system that could deliver water.

If you get this, I mean really get this, the future of your client attraction is going to be transformed.

26

Dealing with Vampires Who Bring You Down

Take a look at your environment—the field of thoughts, actions, and people you put around yourself every day. We tend to become like those with whom we surround ourselves. That's why it's important that you start paying attention to everything and everyone around you.

If you spend your time around grateful people, you will tend to see the world through a lens that leads to you being more grateful. If you spend your time around big thinkers and doers, you will tend to be motivated to do the same or better. We can't really help that this happens. It just does.

If you want to achieve a level of success and freedom most people talk about but never get, then you should understand you don't have to do it alone. There are plenty of others who want to achieve, who want to dream, and who want to succeed. The problem is they're probably not living next door.

When you surround yourself with people who are going places and doing things, you can take on this energy and use it to fuel your own journey. It works. You just know. You know what it feels like to be inspired, empowered, and encouraged by people who share similar goals and by people who motivate you to stretch yourself and grow.

My point is to make sure you get a regular dose of positive people in your life. This habit will make your journey far more pleasant. The fact is, you don't have to tolerate people in your world who bring you down. Respect yourself enough to simply say, "No." You don't have to have an attitude about it. You usually don't even have to say anything out loud. You just have to slowly and methodically begin to remove these situations from your life.

As the amount of positive energy, thought, and action fills your mind and body, you'll tend to attract more of that. The complainers, whiners, and cynics will start to fall away. Let them do that.

27

Commit to YOUR Dreams

In a perfect world, this wouldn't have to be a conversation I'd have to have with you. However, we're not living in a perfect world, so I want to address it here in a direct way.

Until you fully commit to your dreams, you will not have the internal alignment required to fully realize your potential. In other words, you will be leaving a good part of your greatness on the table.

There are lots of reasons people don't commit to their dreams. One reason is that you've probably been told most of your life to be realistic, to just follow the rules and choose a path through life that is safe and secure. First of all, there IS no safe and secure path through life. Life is a risk. Breathing is a risk. Waking up in the morning is a risk. Everything is a risk. That's why life is so valuable.

Another reason people don't commit to their dreams is that they've allowed themselves to be brainwashed that "following your dreams" is something reserved for **OTHER** people to do. Steve Jobs, creator of Apple Computer, knew this wasn't true. Here's what he said:

"When you grow up you tend to get told the world is the way it is, and your life is just to live your life inside the world. Try not to bash into the walls too much. Try to have a nice family, have fun, save a little money. That's a very limited life. Life can be much broader once you discover one simple fact: Everything around you that you call life was made up by people that were no smarter than you and you can change it, you can influence it, you can build your own things that other people can use. Once you learn that, you'll never be the same again."

There's one more big reason people don't commit to their dreams—one more reason that they allow their entire lives to go by without fully engaging with those things that make their hearts sing. People are scared to death of going after their dreams with every ounce of themselves and falling short in front of the whole world. If you "fail," your family will see you. Your friends will see you. All those people who said you were crazy will see you. The truth will be out there for everyone to see. My guess is that some people would rather die than go through this embarrassment.

That's why they never even try. That's why they go through life without ever truly living. This one comes down to a simple choice. Are you going to take a chance on **YOU** and your happiness in life, or are you going to play it safe and ensure you fail by not even trying?

Are you worth it to take a risk on you? That's a question only you can answer. I know the answer, but I can't make you believe it. You have to do the work to get there on your own. In the meanwhile, why not just commit to the dreams you have and get to work? You can always change your mind later if too many of your dreams start coming true.

Below is a powerful quote by Johann Wolfgang von Goethe that you can print and hang where you'll see it every day:

"Until one is committed, there is hesitancy, the chance to draw back, always ineffectiveness. Concerning all acts of initiative and creation, there is one elementary truth the ignorance of which kills countless ideas and splendid plans: that the moment one definitely commits oneself, then providence moves too. All sorts of things occur to help one that would never otherwise have occurred. A whole stream of events issues from the decision, raising in one's favor all manner of unforeseen incidents, meetings and material assistance which no man could have dreamed would have come his way. Whatever you can do or dream you can, begin it. Boldness has genius, power and magic in it. Begin it now."

28

Giving Is a Sign of POWER, Not a Sign of Weakness

There's a terrible trend that's already spread throughout our industry. I have no idea why this is, but I'm not afraid to call it out and steer you away from it.

The reason is that it's the exact opposite of what you should be doing if you want to live the Million Dollar Stylist® lifestyle. What is this horrible thing? At the core of it, it's fear, but on the surface, it looks more like this....

Hairstylists who are scared to give away their "secrets" will not win in the long run. FYI... they are going to lose, and they are going to lose big! If you're scared to give away your secrets, then you are fighting a losing battle.

This approach shouts out to the world loudly and clearly that you are operating in a scarcity mindset. Do you know what happens when you do that? You get scarcity all over the place!

Even more, an unwillingness to give broadcasts to the entire world that you do not feel valuable. It tells everyone that you think you need secrets to make it in the world. If you're going to come along with me on this journey to your biggest success, make a commitment right now that you are not going to participate in this kind of backwards thinking.

Giving is a sign of **power**, not weakness. I know that is true at such a deep level that I base almost everything else I do on it. It works. Trust me.

29

Busy Is Not the Goal–Success is the Goal

There's a valuable book I recommend that you read. It's called *Essentialism* by Greg McKeown. This book really could transform your life, if you allow it. And that transformation could happen with you doing far less than you're probably doing right now.

Many years ago, I had nothing. No business, no money, nothing. Fast-forward to now and my life is very different. If there's one thing I didn't know back then that I surely know now, it is this....

There is a big difference between being successful and just being busy. On TV and in the movies, "successful" people are busy. They've got every minute of their calendar packed to the brim. They literally have zero minutes available for anything or anyone else.

While that might make for a good movie, it makes for a miserable life. To me, success isn't about being busy. There are plenty of successful people who are stuck on their own hamster wheel. They have to keep running and running or the whole thing falls apart. At least, that's what they think. Remember, you can make a deliberate and conscious choice about what you want.

Do you want to be busy or do you want true success? If you feel overwhelmed, I recommend that you pick up a copy of *Essentialism* and put it into practice. If you want to feel what freedom feels like, that book will show you a way to experience it immediately.

I'm going to reveal one of his secrets, though, before we go. It's something that a lot of people are really terrible at doing. If you're terrible at it, too, don't worry. You've been trained to be terrible at it. In other words, you've been trained to be terrible.

What am I talking about? I'm talking about the ability to say... NO.

Your journey to become a Million Dollar Stylist® will speed up to the extent that you develop the ability to say no to the things that do not move you forward. This is hard for a lot of people because, frankly, most people are kind. Saying no when someone asks you to do something or when they offer you an opportunity... well, that can feel awkward.

So, to avoid that feeling, we end up saying "yes" even though we really shouldn't. Add up a bunch of yeses, and pretty soon you get bogged down helping other people build their dreams while your dreams get forgotten. Let me make this really clear so that you really get this at a very deep level.

You can either spend your life building **your** dreams, or you can spend your life building the dreams of others. The path you walk down is determined by the choices that you make. This gets more important the more successful you become. Because once you start to get attention, the opportunities come flying your way. However, you have to stay true to yourself. Ask yourself these questions. What do you want? Where are you trying to go?

How many things in your life and business are you caught up in right now because you didn't say **no** when you should have? If you want to be a Million Dollar Stylist®, this is a skill you will must master. Otherwise, you'll end up running around like a crazy person. You might be able to keep up for a while, but eventually it's going to wear you down.

You'll start to lose your focus, and you'll wonder why you're so busy with so little to show for it. Get clear, get focused, and get to work. Remember, it's about doing **LESS** and doing it better.

30

Build the New, Starve the Old

What you give your attention to tends to get bigger. If you start putting energy towards the things you don't want, you're actually working against yourself. Here's an old Cherokee parable that gets to the heart of what this step is about. In this parable, a Cherokee Chief is teaching his grandson about life:

"A fight is going on inside me," he said to the boy. "It is a terrible fight and it is between two wolves."

"One is evil—he is anger, envy, sorrow, regret, greed, arrogance, self-pity, guilt, resentment, inferiority, lies, false pride, superiority, self-doubt, and ego."

"The other is good—he is joy, peace, love, hope, serenity, humility, kindness, benevolence, empathy, generosity, truth, compassion, and faith."

"This same fight is going on inside you—and inside every other person, too."

The grandson thought about it for a minute and then asked his grandfather, "Which wolf will win?"

The old chief simply replied, "The one you feed."

The point is that what you feed grows. If you feed fear, it will grow. If you feed joy, it will grow. If you feed bad habits, they will grow. If you feed good habits, they will grow. Therefore, the smartest way to transform yourself is to stop focusing on all of those old parts you don't want anymore. You simply move your focus towards building the new.

Eventually, the old will fall away, and you'll look back one day and realize it is no longer there. I can't really expect you to believe me if you haven't experienced it, but it is truly my prayer that you will get to go through this transformation someday. It is an amazing feeling. The journey to build new habits—useful and helpful habits—is exactly that: a journey. You will not be done today. You will not be done tomorrow.

The best way forward is to take one step at a time. When you wake up tomorrow, you take another step, then another. To your mind, this "never-ending journey" is NOT going to sound exciting. You might actually freak out when you think about it! And most likely, your mind will do everything in its power to sabotage your way. It'll start telling you that you won't make it. It'll start saying you can't do it—that people like you just aren't cut out for this.

Just watch and listen to that voice without resistance. Don't fight it. Don't try to prove it wrong. That only strengthens the power it has over you. Instead, simply stop feeding it. Stop giving it attention. Remove your focus from it. Soon enough, it will wither away from lack of attention. One day, it will just disappear. Trust God and don't feed the negative.

31

How to Transform Negativity into Fuel

You transform negativity into fuel by shifting your perspective. Instead of looking at criticism and negativity as problems, we are going to rewire our brains to perceive them as clues. These are clues that show you something important. What is it that they show you?

These are clues that you are actually doing work important enough to touch someone at a deep level. When you do that, people either tend to love you or experience some not so pleasant emotions towards you. In other words, pursuing success tends to polarize people into two camps: those who are rooting for you and those who are rooting against you.

The simple truth is this: if you're not getting criticized, then you aren't yet doing something important enough. As crazy as this line of thinking might feel to you now, stick with me. It's going to get even crazier! Because once you begin to shift your perception of negativity from being a problem to being a clue, you can take the next step and view it as an opportunity.

It's an opportunity for gratitude. You are actually going to develop the ability to be grateful for it. Now before you think I'm off my rocker, I'm not going to leave you hanging there. I'm going to connect these dots for you so you get this. When you get this and start living it, your entire life will change. That is something I can **guarantee**.

At face value, the statement I just made about being grateful for negativity sounds completely crazy, but it's not—not if you are on the Million Dollar Stylist® journey. Bad things are going to happen and are going to be said about you. That is reality. It's your state of mind that determines whether this reality pushes you forward or slows you down.

Negativity directed at you is an opportunity because it serves as a clue that you are doing something worthy of criticism. You are doing something that is clear enough to generate a strong response from someone else. This is an enormous opportunity. Remember, we were trained to avoid negativity and criticism. In fact, most people will betray themselves simply to be liked and accepted by others. This isn't natural. It is a learned behavior.

The reason our school system is set up in its current configuration is because our school system was designed to produce people who could work long hours doing boring things. Long before school became mandatory, most kids worked at home in their parents' business or farm. In that environment, you didn't have to sit and do one thing forever. However, when the factories came along, that's the skill the factory owners needed. They needed people who could sit still, follow directions, not ask too many questions, and stand in line. They created the school system to teach those skills to their future workers.

When you have your own business, the rules are completely different. That's why school doesn't prepare you for life—not any life that a Million Dollar Stylist® wants to live—that's for sure. In business, negativity is a form of clarity. It is actually a valuable thing, not a bad thing. The long-term goal here is to undo the brainwashing you got when you were a kid and get your head screwed on straight for success.

When you're selling something or selling yourself, you want a **YES** or a **NO**. Either one will work. What doesn't work is an "I don't know." That helps no one. You get a YES or a NO when you are clear. When it's clear to someone whether or not you belong in their life, that makes your decisions easier. Negativity is just a clear NO. That's just as valid as a YES, as long as we don't let our training and brainwashing tell us differently. It also serves as a reminder to refocus on the destination you are moving towards.

For most people, the negative stuff that shows up (a bad book review, an annoyed customer, a client who spreads rumors about you) grows and grows and grows until the poor person can't see anything else. Progress completely grinds to a halt. That single issue pushes everything else out of their field of vision. The path forward is blocked by this huge issue they have blown way out of proportion. For the Million Dollar Stylist®, things are different. Million Dollar Stylists® are prepared for this.

We know what to do to minimize the delay this negative garbage creates in our journey. What stops others cold becomes like a fly on the windshield for us. Bad things come and bad things go, but they don't affect where our car is going! Get out of the way. We're coming through!

You may wonder if negativity is really an opportunity. Of course, it is. Everything is. Everything that happens is an opportunity for you to make a choice. You can choose to respond in a way that makes you grow and move forward, or you can choose to respond in a way that makes you get smaller and move backwards. Everything that happens to you is an opportunity for this decision.

We each get to make this decision hundreds, maybe thousands, of times a day. The reason you develop a state of being that allows you to be grateful for these opportunities is because the feeling of gratitude you feel is something that helps you recognize the abundance that is all around you. You recognize the abundance, even when things aren't exactly as you want them to be, even when the money is tight; even when the relationships are strained; and even when the clients are slow in showing up.

When you are in this state, you become attractive to many more good things. It all begins with a choice. **The good news is that you have complete control over this choice**. The skill you want to develop is the ability to make the right choice (the one that moves you forward) no matter what is happening in your life.

Whew! That's a lot of deep stuff to wade through. Just take it one step at a time. You're going to be amazed at what happens as you put this into practice.

32

The Plan "C" Secret

The "Plan C Secret" means you get in the habit of thinking, "What's next on my agenda if this plan doesn't work?" It means you don't get in the lazy habit of putting all your eggs in one basket.

We all know what happens when you trip over a rock and one basket goes flying. No eggs for you!

Sit down and start to get ideas about ways you can add brand new income streams to your business. From experience, I can tell you it's a great feeling when no **ONE** particular thing you do **HAS** to work out. When you have several things going on at once, you can see which things work out and then discard the rest. It's a much less stressful way to live.

Start with taking a clear look at your business today. How many streams of revenue are flowing into your world? What would have to change for you to double that, triple it, 20x it? At this point in the process, please, whatever you do, don't allow your mind to shoot down even the most outlandish ideas you come up with.

EVERYTHING is on the table. Make sure you're prepared to write down all the ideas that come to you. Then, start working on making ONE new income stream a reality. Is it a new product? Is it a new service you're going to offer? Is it a completely new type of client you're going to attract? Don't be afraid to say what you want and then go after it.

If you don't want to work behind a chair any more than you already are, then don't go looking to double your client base. Look for ways to generate new revenue streams without needing more clients.

Diversifying is not a one-time event. While it would be cool to just wave a magic wand and have it all done once and for all, that's just not realistic. Diversifying is a process and a new way of thinking that you will practice, improve, and practice again. It's never done! The best time to start doing this is five years ago. The second-best time is <u>NOW</u>. Make this a priority for you. Make you and your future well-being a priority for you.

If you're truly going to help the world, then you have to put yourself on solid ground so you can focus on helping others.

I want to make one last point regarding diversification. Many people do it all wrong. They start businesses completely unrelated to their current business—one that's already working. My advice is to start businesses and income streams very closely related to what is already making money for you. This way, when one business is doing well, your other businesses or streams of income will naturally do better because they are feeding each other. More importantly, when one of your businesses gets a new customer, it's nice to be able to sell that same customer other products and services that are complimentary. It makes everything so much easier for you, and it gives your customer additional products and services they'll love while you control the flow of those products and services.

33

The Most Valuable Asset In Your Business

If you had to name the most valuable asset in your entire business, what would it be?

I'll accept two right answers here, but my hunch is you won't guess either. Think about it. What's the most valuable thing in your entire business?

If you said the tools you use in your business to work with clients, that's strike one! If you said your skills doing hair, that's strike two! Those are not the answers at the top of my mind. If you said your clients, you're getting closer. But you're still not there. I'll give you one more guess.... Give up? OKAY.

The answer is actually something I guarantee not 1 in 1,000 stylists would guess. It's not because stylists aren't smart; it's because no one ever tells you just how important this part of your business is.

You are one of the most important assets in your business, but I want to go even deeper. There are two that are paramount to success. The first one is your list of clients, prospective clients, customers, and prospective customers. The second is the relationship that exists with all those people. The real asset is the list. It's really gold, if you think about it.

Ask the average stylist, "How big is your list?" and I guarantee they will look at you like you've just gone nuts. Most likely, all you'll get in response is them saying, "What list?" And that, dear reader, is one of the biggest competitive advantages you will have on your journey to living the Million Dollar Stylist® lifestyle. You will know the true secret to this type of business.

The list is the #1 asset in your business that's going to make a lot of wonderful things possible for you.

Most stylists operate under a "hope and pray" type of arrangement. They hope and pray that new clients come in the door. This is a terrible strategy. It makes you feel terrible, too, because every day, when you wake up, you are pretty much at the mercy of chance. That doesn't feel good at all.

I'm here to tell you that you can be much smarter about this. You can be one of the only stylists in your area who tosses out the hope and pray strategy and actually has a plan and process in place for creating the life and business you want.

This is a complicated topic, but you can start simply. First, start collecting the information (e-mail address, physical address, cell phone, etc.) of your clients. Imagine the next time you want to earn a certain amount of money or want to take your family on a vacation. Wouldn't it be easier to make that happen if you had 1,000 former clients to send a simple e-mail or text about a special promotion you are having?

You're doing the hard work to make clients happy. Make sure you're building the list of those people in a way where YOU can reach out to them.

Here's a true story to illustrate my point. We had a client who is a doctor. He wanted to generate an extra $40,000 the next month for a certain project he was working on. What we did was pull his local customer database and export all the customer names.

Then, we created a $3,995 offer for 10 people only. We created an amazing offer that was worth roughly $10,000, but we discounted it to $3,995 and created a deadline to join. By creating this amazing offer, limiting it to just 10 people, and discounting the way we did, we sold all 10 within a week and our client was thrilled.

The point is, none of this could have happened without the customer's information. Never underestimate the value of your customer database or your relationship with your customers.

34

How to Deal With Your Biggest Fan

As challenging as it might be to become a Million Dollar Stylist®, you will have help along the way. You'll have all of the help we provide for you here, you'll have help and encouragement from the people you surround yourself with, and you'll also have help from your "fans."

If you've been in business for any length of time, you already have fans. Those are the people that love what you do and how you do it. But there is one fan who will be with you for this entire journey. I call this person your "biggest fan." That person is **YOU**.

Most people don't think of themselves as their biggest fan. We were all taught not to be proud, not to brag, not to be arrogant, not to be boastful. While it's smart not to be those things, that doesn't mean you can't be confident, grateful, and in awe of the things you do.

In fact, in order to make it on this journey, you must dig deep into your core and figure out where all your confidence is hiding. You want to become your own biggest fan. You want to become your own encouragement and support. You want to become your own cheerleader.

When you are able to do that, you are able to give to yourself what you will need for your journey. Remember, there's a big difference between confidence and bragging. Look to God for joy, security, and growth. However, never forget that you have free will and a beating heart. Be thankful you're alive and go into the world and represent yourself in a positive way with great confidence. The people around you are counting on you.

35

Head Trash

You've got to realize just how valuable you truly are. Read that sentence again. This time, pay close attention to what your mind chatter does as you read that. If you're anything like most people, reading a sentence like this is going to bring up some interesting thoughts like these....

» Now don't go getting a big head. No one likes someone who brags.

» You're not that special. A lot of people could do what you do.

» "Pride goeth before a fall."

» Special? You? Are you serious?

» What would your mother or father say about this? Don't you remember they always told you to be humble?

And people wonder why they have a hard time getting through life. How could you **not** have a hard time with thoughts like **these** running through your head?

The first step in caring for your biggest fan (You!) is to develop the ability to appreciate and be grateful for just how valuable you are. This doesn't mean you can't do the same for others. It just means you must be sure not to forget to do it for yourself too! This is a process, not an event, so don't expect to reverse years of brainwashing in just a minute. This is a daily decision to make.

Ask yourself this question: Do you show up **today** as your best self or not?

The next step is to begin giving yourself the right fuel for your journey. You've got to feed your mind, body, and spirit. You can't ignore any one of these parts and expect to fulfill your potential. How often do you feed your mind? How often do you give it the nourishment it needs to grow beautiful and powerful ideas?

Despite what scientists probably say, I view the mind as a muscle. The more you use it, the more powerful it becomes. That's why I'm always feeding my mind. I invest in training myself. I invest in mentors. I invest in the knowledge I need to grow. I feed my mind A LOT so I can turn around and help feed the minds of Million Dollar Stylists® across the world.

Then there's the body. What you put in your body is the fuel you get for your journey. Put good stuff in and you have good fuel. Put bad stuff in and you won't. It's as simple as that. Care for your body and it will care for you.

And, of course, there is spirit. There are many ways to care for your spirit. No matter what that means for you, the goal is to NOT allow this part of you to get pushed down on your "to do" list. This connection is the most important part of the whole recipe. It's easy to feel when this connection is missing. When my connection to God is being ignored by me, I feel it everywhere. Life turns into a bizarre gray and it loses its vividness. Consider this your reminder to make sure that you don't ignore this part of your life!

It's a big responsibility to walk on the road toward success. Two of the biggest jobs are dealing with your head trash and giving yourself everything you need to fuel your journey.

36

Have, Do, Be

Tell me if this line of thinking make sense to you:

"If I could only have more money, then I'd have more time to do the things that could help me be more successful." I'm going to write that sentence again, but this time I'm going to highlight a few important words: If I could only *have* more money, then I'd *have* more time to *do* the things that could help me *be* more successful. The important words I highlighted are HAVE, DO, BE.

If that sentence makes sense to you, then congratulations! You're in good company because that's how most of the world views things. If they could only have, then they could do, then they could be.

As it turns out, this is exactly the OPPOSITE way of how it really works. To understand why, here's a short parable about a Mexican fisherman. I don't know who wrote it, so I can't give credit to the author. Read it. Then I'll see you on the other side of the story.

An American investment banker was at the pier of a small coastal Mexican village when a small boat with just one fisherman docked. Inside the small boat were several large yellowfin tunas. The American complimented the Mexican on the quality of his fish and asked how long it took to catch them.

The Mexican replied, "only a little while." The American then asked why he didn't stay out longer and catch more fish. The Mexican said he had enough to support his family's immediate needs. The American then asked, "But what do you do with the rest of your time?"

The Mexican fisherman said, "I sleep late, fish a little, play with my children, take siestas with my wife, Maria, stroll into the village each evening where I sip wine, and play guitar with my amigos. I have a full and busy life."

The American scoffed. "I am a Harvard MBA and could help you. You should spend more time fishing and with the proceeds, buy a bigger boat. With the proceeds from the bigger boat, you could buy several boats. Eventually you would have a fleet of fishing boats.

Instead of selling your catch to a middleman you would sell directly to the processor, eventually opening your own cannery. You would control the product, processing, and distribution.

You would need to leave this small coastal fishing village and move to Mexico City, then LA, and eventually New York City, where you will run your expanding enterprise."

The Mexican fisherman asked, "But, how long will this all take?"

To which the American replied, "15 - 20 years." "But what then?" asked the Mexican. The American laughed and said, "That's the best part. When the time is right you would announce an IPO and *sell your company stock to the public and become very rich, you would make millions!"*

"Millions—then what?"

The American said, "Then you would retire. Move to a small coastal fishing village where you would sleep late, fish a little, play with your kids, take siestas with your wife, stroll to the village in the evenings where you could sip wine and play your guitar with your amigos."

Be, Do, Have

The parable is a cool story, but it's also extremely true. The way to be successful is NOT to believe in the "have, do, be" path. The truth is that you must BE the person you want to be, and then start doing the types of things that person would do. That is when you enjoy HAVING the things that type of person has.

You really want to think about this because it can unlock so many doors for you in your business and your life. Not only that, but it will keep you from getting frustrated along the way. When you know the true source of all success (which I describe as knowing who you have to BECOME), then it makes the journey a very different type of journey.

It's something you can actually enjoy instead of something you try to get through. Be, Do, Have is an enormous secret.

When you can figure out WHO you have to be and WHO you want to be, then the doing and the having pretty much take care of themselves.

37

Stop Trying to Get Clients

The Platform is an important piece in your system for attracting clients. Average stylist thinking puts your focus on the CLIENT as the real asset in your business. Clients are important, but you have to look at things differently. The client is not the asset.... The system that attracts the client is the real asset that you build. It is an asset that will increase in value over time.

On one hand, this is simple for any stylist to understand. Unfortunately, most stylists will go through their entire careers never ONCE thinking about things this way. And that's why they will work hard—forever—just to make ends meet.

You will be different, however, because your focus will be on building the SYSTEM that attracts the clients. Your platform is the keystone of your entire client attraction system.

Yes, it's work. REAL work. But it's work that is leveraged. What that means is that you do the work once and then reap the benefit over and over again. This is the pipeline approach. Do work ONCE, receive benefit FOREVER. In my book, *Fully Booked*, I go really deep into the power of a system like this.

Here's a short excerpt from the book:

My recommendation to you right now is to stop trying to get clients. You read that right.

Stop investing energy and focus on something you do not control. Instead, we're going to focus all of that energy on something you actually do control. Something that will actually bring the clients without you trying to get them! We're going to use "Oprah's Secret" to attract clients to your salon.

The secret is the Platform. What is it? It can be a lot of things. For Oprah, it was her TV show. For me, it's a podcast, videos, e-mails, and more. Even this book! For you, it could be a newsletter, a video blog, an audio/video podcast, or something else. Here's why it works and what makes it so valuable.

Attracting clients is not a one-time event. Like I said earlier, you don't attract clients when you need them. You attract clients all the time! Before a client decides to come to your salon and sit in your chair, a few things have to be true:

#1: They Must Know You Exist
#2: They Must Know You Are Skilled
#3: They Must Trust You

So how do you go about making sure those things happen?

Well, you can't really just come out and say it. Stylists who do that just end up being annoying. Needing to "convince" a client that you are awesome makes you look NOT-awesome. The answer to my question is the Platform. The Platform is what communicates all of these things to your prospective clients over time.

The Platform is a DEMONSTRATION tool. Think back to Oprah again. If you've ever seen her on TV or even on the Internet, what is she doing? Well, some people would watch and say, "She's a great interviewer...." That would certainly be one obvious answer. But it's more than that. What she's actually doing is providing a demonstration of what she is about.

Day after day... more demonstration. Eventually, you begin to trust someone like that. Eventually, you begin to see just how skilled and talented that person is. Eventually, you realize that this person is for you! I have to say, I am so excited to see what amazing things get created when these strategies get into the hands of stylists all over the world.

The only requirement is that you have to be willing to do the work. You have to become valuable for people FIRST.

38

Tune Your Signal

Clarity is everything. As the Cheshire Cat in Alice in Wonderland says, "If you don't know where you're going, any road'll take you there." It sure will.

The habit you want to develop is the ability to get clearer and clearer about exactly what you want. The trick is to make sure this answer is YOUR answer. Our culture is obsessed with making you want what others have. That's not a recipe for long-term success. That's a recipe for failure. Tune into what you want.

For some people, once they get their answer they stick with it. For others, it's a moving target. For a little while, success looks like X to them; then it looks like Y. Changing your mind isn't a problem.

Making sure you remember to check in with yourself about whether the direction you're going is STILL the road you want to travel is the habit you need to develop. Otherwise, you risk investing a lot of time and effort doing things that aren't going to pay off for you.

Habit #1 is to remember to get clear, stay clear, and adjust so you know what you want. That makes every decision you make much easier.

39

You're a Loser!

The immediate benefit of the "expect nothing" attitude is that you won't be frustrated every morning when you wake up expecting X to happen only to find that it didn't happen. However, there's another benefit—one that's even more powerful.

The big benefit is that when you expect nothing, everything good that does happen is something for which you can be extremely grateful. Now I don't know exactly why this works, but I know it does work. What I'm talking about is that magic seems to happen when you go through life being grateful for everything. There's something miraculous about having that feeling in your body. It does amazing things out in the world.

Be grateful in all things. I know, that's easier said than done, but it CAN be done. And it's really the shortcut to becoming an enormously powerful Million Dollar Stylist®. The power of gratitude will transform your future.

Expecting nothing doesn't mean you're not working your butt off. It doesn't mean you're not doing your best. It doesn't mean you're not focused on success. Expecting nothing is not an excuse for being lazy. It is a recipe for happiness. The real secret here is that you are developing the habit of not getting emotionally attached to a specific result happening at a specific time from a specific person.

Just think about all the times in your life where you've caused yourself pain or frustration by thinking things should be other than they actually are. "I really should have more clients. I really should charge more for my services. I really should have more people paying attention to me. Arrggggghhhh!" Those are frustrating situations. They're even more frustrating when you don't accept them.

Whatever position you're in right now, OWN IT. That's where you're at. Don't complain about it. Just take a step forward and keep going. When you stop getting emotionally attached to what is or is not happening in your life and business, you will experience true freedom. Watch out if you've never felt that before. It's an amazing feeling.

40

"You're Fat! You're Ugly. You Have No Talent."

The fact is, the world is filled with good and bad, light and dark. You can't have one without the other. On your Million Dollar Stylist® journey, you're going to get both. I can't guarantee much on this journey, but I can guarantee that!

That means you have a choice: you can either prepare yourself to deal with both sides of reality or you can suffer when the "you know what" hits the fan. When that nasty comment hits your page about how your work is mediocre, you can choose whether to let it bother you or fuel you. When that customer wants her money back because your product was "trash," you can choose to have it ruin your day (or week!) or give you immediate clarity about how to help more people in better ways. When that trusted friend starts spreading rumors online about you, you can choose to have it take you down or propel you higher.

Here's the challenge: we've been trained to deal with the negativity that enters our lives in ways that are not productive. We get trained to react this way in school. We get trained to react this way by our family and friends. Can you remember when the teacher in school singled people out and "made an example" of them? It doesn't really matter if those kids deserved it or not. The result of the training was the same: most of us will immediately feel BAD when someone says or does something negative towards us.

"You're fat! You're ugly. You have no talent. You will get NOWHERE in life. You'll NEVER make it." Can you imagine someone saying all this nasty stuff to you?

I don't have to imagine it. I've had stuff like this happen. And the funny thing is, the more success I create, the more it happens! It's crazy!

How do you deal with it? You prepare for it so that when it shows up, you are ready. That way, when it happens to you (and if you're doing this Million Dollar Stylist® thing right, it WILL happen), you won't miss a beat. In fact, you'll gather power from it instead of having it knock you off your center.

The first step in dealing with any negativity that comes at you from the outside world is to remember that it is RARELY, if ever, actually about you. That might sound crazy to say, but I'm 100% serious. When someone points the finger at you and hurls some insult or criticism your way, it says far more about them than anything about you. Let me explain what I mean.

Right now, much of humanity is not in a good place. They want what they don't have; they don't like what they do have. They have broken dreams, a bunch of unresolved emotional baggage, and loads of anger and angst about why their lives aren't the way they should be. The bottom line here is that most people are experiencing pain on many levels. When someone lashes out at you, it's usually because they simply can't bear to keep their own pain from spilling out.

When you view things with this type of understanding, you realize these negative folks are not out to get you. They are simply in pain and doing the best they can. When you show up on their radar, you become a convenient target for them to release some pain. They see the target (you) and they shoot. Isn't that unfair? Isn't it unfair that someone would unload on you simply because they can't bear to hold it in anymore? I don't believe in fair or unfair. I believe in reality and responding to what is with POWER.

This is not a common opinion, I admit, but I haven't found a better way to go through life. I also don't believe in playing the victim (EVER) just because someone is having a bad day... so I don't. I'd recommend you never play the victim role, either. It robs you of the power you have to move forward and grow.

Instead, I do my best to meet this negative garbage with compassion. It probably sounds like I'm totally crazy, so let me break this down for you: If you sit with this long enough, you can actually develop a certain level of compassion for the people who do this to you. That doesn't mean you become a doormat so they can walk all over you.

It just means that you can actually develop empathy for the type of being who is experiencing so much pain that their only relief is to spread it to someone else.

This is Step #1: Develop the ability to simply watch that negative crap come at you. Don't react to it. Don't go crazy about it. Just sit with it and be still for a moment. Then just breathe. That really helps. Just keep breathing, even if you are upset at the moment. There's power in breathing and usually when something crazy happens, that's the first thing that gets interrupted. Don't let that happen. Just go right to deep breathing, and keep at it until you calm down on the inside.

Now, understand that everything I'm walking you through isn't about AVOIDING the negative stuff that comes with success. There is no avoiding it. In fact, it's probably going to increase. However, you won't care, not if you've committed to doing the work. That's a key thing to remember. Negativity isn't something you wait to deal with only when it happens. It's something you prepare for so that when it does happen, it just rolls right on by.

41

The Most Valuable Use of Your Time

Despite what you've been told in school, the most valuable activity you can possibly engage in is THINKING.

Yes, action is important, but let me ask you this question. What informs the actions you take and the actions you don't take?

It's the quality of your thinking. If you want to improve your business, improve the level of thinking that goes into your business.

I wish I could offer a silver bullet that would make this easy, but I don't have one. It's just like everything else: the more you practice it, the better you get, except thinking isn't something that's linear. If you move up a level in your thinking, you don't get double your results. The growth is more exponential, so you might get something like 10x the results.

That's why thinking is so important.

How did you get so good at doing hair? Maybe you have talent, of course, but most likely you got really good because you practiced A LOT. You see, I've been doing hair since I was six (if you count my Cabbage Patch Doll)! Granted, I started on a doll, but it was still practice. I practiced for decades. And do you know what? I'm still practicing. I'm never going to stop.

You are here to be valuable to the world. Think about what that should look like. Once you get started, think about it some more.

Practicing this skill will transform your life.

42

The Biggest Secret Ever

It's easy to feel lost in the world of business. Some things work. Some things don't work. There are people who have accomplished more than you could ever dream to do. You can let this get to you, or you can just accept it as reality.

I'd like to take this opportunity to let you in on a little secret about all of those people you admire, about all those folks you look up to, about all those folks who you might wish you could be. This is a secret I certainly didn't know when I started out, and I doubt 1 out of 1,000 people are truly aware of it.

The secret is this: **I don't care what famous or successful person you're talking about, there's a good chance they feel like they don't know what they're doing.** You know how—when you're learning to speak in front of groups of people—they tell you to imagine everyone without clothes on, just so you can lighten up and not be so nervous? I'm talking about the same dynamic but on a deeper level.

If you feel like you're a little bit lost, like you're not sure you can make it out there, like you don't know what to do next... just know that most EVERYONE else feels this way too. This is not a bad thing. In fact, I think it's a great thing.

First of all, it keeps you humble. It keeps you very well aware that you can always learn more, that you can always get better at doing what you do. Second, it keeps you from getting lazy. It keeps your mind engaged and focused on the goals you are trying to achieve.

Finally, when you realize that no one knows what they are doing, you can begin to understand the depth of your creative power. You have the power to create your life and reality as you see fit. Best of all, you can eventually get to a point where you say, "If they can do it, then there's no reason I can't do it too!"

Then you can get about the work of transforming your life and the lives of others. This is an important moment. It's the one where you finally BELIEVE that people no smarter than you have done great things.

It's one thing to understand this in your mind; it's quite another thing to feel it in your core, but it's the truth.

43

Elephants for Dinner

How do you eat an elephant? As the saying goes, you eat it one bite at a time. When you're dealing with habits, it's exciting to think that your life is going to be completely different tomorrow if you just "fix these 12 things."

If you've ever tried this, you know it doesn't last. You get all excited one day about the new life you've decided to live and you're all pumped up. Yeah! Then life happens, the weeks go by, and you just run out of steam. If you do this too many times, you might even start to believe that you're just STUCK and that you'll never make the changes you want.

You change big things by first changing the small things. It's a little like a snowball rolling down the hill. At one point, there's ONE snowflake in that snowball and it builds from there. Then two, then 20, 100, 1,000,000. After a while the momentum carries you through, even if the journey is hard. That's why trying to change everything at once is not a smart way to go. It's too much.

Let me repeat: Don't try to do it all at once. It's far better that you focus on one thing at a time than to try to focus on everything at once. This is impossible, and it will set you up for some big struggles. Most likely, you'll end up quitting and then just go back to your old ways.

The goal isn't to impress anyone here. The goal is to actually install new habits that move you closer to your goals. That's it. Start slow, stay consistent, and enjoy the ride. If you're serious about installing new habits or getting rid of old habits, just pick one.

It's kind of funny if you're trying to get rid of a bad habit. I've found that one effective way to do it is to override it with a new habit. Instead of saying, "I'm never going to do this again!" you simply start a NEW habit that crowds out the bad one.

What you focus on gets done. Don't water down your power of focus by doing too many things. Pick ONE. Master it. Pick the next ONE. You didn't develop your current habits overnight. They took time and a lot of practice! Be patient and gentle with yourself. Take your time. Take a step. Take another step. Breathe!

44

Growing New Branches on Your Tree

Most stylists "do hair." That's it. Some do weaves, color, and other stuff, of course, but very few stylists step beyond the realm of exchanging money with clients for personal services. In general, most stylists work for money. They do something in exchange for getting money. Now, I'll admit that exchanging money for hair services beats working in a boring office job, but there's a lot more possibility out there for you!

That's why, in the Million Dollar Stylist® world, we create products, offer workshops, and develop brand new services that allow us to deliver more value to our customers and clients without us necessarily being personally involved each time. With each new stream of income we develop, our position in this Million Dollar Stylist® world gets stronger. The foundation becomes more secure, but most stylists never build multiple streams of income.

Here's an excerpt from an e-mail I sent out not long ago. Please read this carefully. I want to make sure to take this opportunity to explain to you JUST HOW SERIOUS this topic is to your future: One of the fastest ways to fail in business is to rely on one source of income.

****

Most people get real comfortable making money a certain type of way and they don't diversify.

This is a mistake.

I've always tried my best to not have any one source of income be more than 33% of my income. It's never perfect, but I try to hit the numbers. Let me make this simple for you.

If you make $10,000 per month doing hair and you're busy 40 hours per week doing weaves and color, good job. But what I would recommend is you start diversifying that $10,000 or add a few more streams to it. If it were me, based on my 33% ratio, I'd want $3,333 coming from hair, $3,333 coming from selling products, and $3,333 from consulting.

It doesn't matter HOW you make it happen, just always be diversifying until you achieve the stability you want. According to most stylists, this is crazy talk. How could anything possibly be "wrong" with making $10K per month doing hair?

There's nothing wrong with it, but it's not ideal. So what happens to your $10K per month income stream the day AFTER you fall off your bike and break your arm? Now I wouldn't wish that on any stylist, but let's be realistic. You can either build your Million Dollar Stylist® world on a strong foundation or you can build it on sand.

So why not just elevate your thinking to a level that allows you to build SMART so you end up with a business that can actually support you instead of forcing you to support IT?

****

Beautiful trees have lots of branches. Start thinking that way, and you will help make sure that all of your hard work goes into building something that will <u>last</u>.

45

Putting It All on the Line and Why Not to Do It

One of the biggest obstacles to doing business the way I'm suggesting is overcoming all the programming you've received about how things are supposed to go. In the movies, the struggling entrepreneur overcomes all challenges to see her big dream become a reality. She puts it all on the line for her dream.

In the movies, everything works out! The challenges go away, the problems get solved, everyone lives happily ever after... except that's a lie.

If you're reading this right now I KNOW you've been in the real world, and you know what the real world can be like.

They don't make movies about the 98% of people chasing their dreams who crash and burn. Who would pay money to see a movie like that? Nobody. They've basically been brainwashing people all these years to follow in the footsteps of the .05% of the people who just have it all work out for them.

Those are the people who got lucky. While that's great for them, it doesn't really help you. I don't know about you but waiting for luck doesn't sound like a risk I'm willing to take with my entire future!

That's why I walk on a much more realistic path. I pursue many different projects because I know that some will work out and some will not. I'm not going to let that reality ruin my chances of reaching my goals.

The mind gets excited when it sees we have a dream. It wants us to live out the story like they do in the movies. It actually pushes us to put all of our eggs in one basket, and give it all we have to pursue our dream!

Remember, take it slow—one step at a time.

You don't have to put it all on the line. You just have to keep moving forward.

46

Tick, Tock, and Time Management

Time management isn't something you do because someone said you should. You don't do it because you heard it was the smart thing to do. You manage your time because you know it is the most valuable asset you possess. When you truly GET THAT, something on the inside will shift forever.

The fact is, time is far more important than money, far more important than connections or status. You don't get any more time than you get. No one knows how much that is. Plan each moment carefully. The real secret to time management isn't making sure you get everything done that you want to get done. It's being aware enough of your time that you don't let unnecessary things get in your way.

Time management is really about keeping unimportant things OUT. It's kind of funny that this is a huge part of the Million Dollar Stylist® journey. You must do a lot of things to get there, but there's a far LONGER list of things you have to make sure you DON'T do. Otherwise, you get stuck and waste tons of time on things that ultimately don't matter much.

What can you cut out? What things are you doing that are not worthy of a piece of your life?

47

Gratitude in All Things

One of the biggest sources of misery in our world is people not being grateful for what they have. Consequently, one of the biggest pitfalls that can slow your Million Dollar Stylist® journey is not developing the habit that allows you to accept WHAT IS.

Look at every area of your life. Are you grateful for every part? Most people aren't. Usually, most of us like some parts and hate other parts. Look at each area of your life and say, "Thank you!" I'm not kidding. I'm suggesting that you develop the habit of being thankful for all of it. Why? I can think of a couple reasons, but I'll highlight the most important one.

In the business world, most people are needy. They need clients, they need money, they need people to like them, and they need life to go the way they want it to go. It's a miserable way to go through life, I know. I imagine you do too. We've all been there. When you develop the habit to be grateful for all things, that neediness goes away. You can't have both. Try it.

There's no way for you to be grateful and needy at the same time. Need attracts more need. Gratitude attracts more reasons for gratitude (aka abundance). Decide which you want more of and do the work required to get it.

There's another reason this habit is important. Before you can change the things in your life and business you want to improve, you have to OWN THEM. You must develop the ability to say, "This is where I'm at, this is where I'm going, and I'm OKAY with all of it." There is great power available to you in OWNING every portion of your life— every decision, every consequence. It makes you attractive to others because, to be frank, most people can't do this. They're scared. The world has taught them NOT to do it. However, not taking responsibility for everything in your life makes you easy to control... and it makes you miserable.

Set yourself free.

OWN it.

Be grateful.

About The Author

Marquetta Breslin is the co-founder of Breslin Products, LLC. She is a Licensed Cosmetologist, educator, and author of *Million Dollar Stylist* and *Fully Booked*. She has educated some of the industry's top professionals, including Oscar-nominated makeup artists and *Vogue Magazine* Editorial Stylists. Marquetta has been featured in *Sophisticate's Black Hair Magazine, BNB, Business 2.0, NBC, CNNMoney.com, NBC,* and *ABC*. Her custom lace wigs have graced celebrities, cancer patients, politicians, and Hollywood feature films. She is the creator of systems such as "Lace Wig Training System," "Cutting Mastery," and "Million Dollar Stylist®," which have reached more than 100,000 customers in more than 70 countries. She is also a professional speaker and trainer, mainly at live events, such as her Lace Wig Mastery Training Seminar and Million Dollar Stylist® LIVE! For booking information, please visit MarquettaBreslin.com.

Notes

Notes

Notes

Notes

Notes